The
Mexican-American War

by Rena Korb

PEARSON
Scott
Foresman

Editorial Offices: Glenview, Illinois • Parsippany, New Jersey • New York, New York

Sales Offices: Needham, Massachusetts • Duluth, Georgia • Glenview, Illinois
Coppell, Texas • Sacramento, California • Mesa, Arizona

During Polk's presidency, the United States gained the right to more land. This land later became the states of Oregon and Washington.

Buildup to War

In the spring of 1846, Mexican armies and United States troops had gathered on opposite sides of the Rio Grande in Texas. The United States claimed that the **boundary**, or border, between the two countries was the Rio Grande. Mexico disagreed.

Mexican soldiers crossed the river and attacked a group of United States soldiers on April 25. On May 13, 1846, the United States declared war against Mexico.

Causes of the War

To understand the causes of the Mexican War, it is important to look at earlier events. Mexico had won its independence from Spain in 1821. Spanish colonies in North America became Mexican **provinces** of New Mexico, California, and Texas. Then settlers from the United States who lived in Texas fought Mexican forces and created their own country. When the United States **annexed** Texas in 1845, the Mexican government was angry. The United States wanted Texas and all the land west to the Pacific Ocean. The idea that the United States should stretch from coast to coast was known as **manifest destiny**.

At the end of March 1846, General Zachary Taylor's troops began building forts along the Rio Grande.

Objections to the War

Not all Americans supported the war with Mexico. Some United States senators believed that the boundary between the two countries was the Nueces River, not the Rio Grande. Also, many people who opposed slavery disliked the war.

In 1845 the United States tried to buy the Mexican land. John Slidell went to Mexico to offer up to $30 million for the purchase of the provinces of New Mexico and California. The Mexican government refused to see Slidell. There seemed little chance of getting the land other than taking it by force. After the battle between the two armies at the Rio Grande, the United States had a reason to go to war.

The Capture of New Mexico

In June 1846 Colonel Stephen Kearney led about 1,500 troops toward New Mexico's capital, Santa Fe. Kearney claimed the towns they passed along the way. On August 18, the troops reached Santa Fe. Kearney raised the American flag and announced that the United States was annexing New Mexico.

Advantages in Fighting the Mexican War

American Advantages	Mexican Advantages
• Better weapons	• Three times more soldiers
• Better military leaders	• Possible aid from Great Britain and France
• Better-trained soldiers	• Disapproval of the war by many Americans

Most New Mexicans accepted United States rule. However, a group of New Mexicans and Pueblo Indians started a **rebellion**. The United States army chased the rebels, and the rebels surrendered. New Mexico was now under the control of the United States.

Colonel Stephen Kearney captured New Mexico from Mexico.

The Bear Flag Revolt was named for the flag the American settlers made that pictured a grizzly bear.

The Bear Flag Revolt

By the summer of 1846, fighting also had broken out in California. California's non-American Indian populations numbered about eight thousand Mexicans, called *Californios*, and five hundred U.S. settlers.

On June 14, a small group of settlers in Sonoma arrested the Mexican army commander and captured military weapons. Then they wrote their declaration of independence from Mexico. They named California the Bear Flag Republic.

United States troops held off a Mexican attack in the Battle of San Gabriel in California.

The Capture of California

United States Navy troops landed on the coast in July. Soldiers took over land held by the *Californios*. After about a month, United States forces thought they had control of California. However, the *Californios* rebelled and by mid-December had regained most of southern California. About that time, Colonel Kearney and his army arrived in San Diego. They marched toward Los Angeles and put down the rebellion in January. The United States had captured California.

The War in Mexico

While some United States troops were fighting in the northern provinces, others invaded Mexico. General Taylor earned his first major victory on May 18, 1846. He captured the town of Matamoros on the other side of the Rio Grande. Taylor then raised the American flag over the town.

Before he crossed the Rio Grande, General Taylor had led his troops into several successful battles against the Mexican army.

The Battles of Monterrey and Buena Vista

In September 1846, Taylor led his soldiers to Monterrey. Monterrey was guarded by several hills that had forts on top of them. United States troops captured the forts and entered the city. After several days of fighting, the Mexicans gave up.

The battle for Monterrey had weakened both armies. The armies agreed to stop fighting for eight weeks. In January 1847, a force of about twenty thousand Mexican troops tried to retake Monterrey. When Taylor learned of the planned attack, he led his five thousand men to nearby Buena Vista. After a few days of hard fighting, neither side appeared close to a victory. American troops expected another fierce struggle on the third morning of the Battle of Buena Vista. To their surprise, they awoke to find the Mexican troops had gone.

United States troops scrambled up the hills of Monterrey.

Today, Mexicans remember several cadets who fought at Chapultepec as los Niños Héroes, or "the Boy Heroes."

The Capture of Veracruz

Many U.S. military leaders believed they needed to capture Mexico City. About ten thousand American troops landed on the coast near the city of Veracruz. They blasted the city with cannonballs. Mexican soldiers returned fire. Within a few days, the cannonballs had blown a hole in the town wall. The city fell to American troops on March 27, 1847.

The Capture of Mexico City

One week later, American soldiers began the long march to Mexico City. They defeated all the Mexican forces that tried to stop them. They attacked an old castle that was used as a Mexican military school. On September 14, 1847, United States forces entered Mexico City.

The Treaty of Guadalupe Hidalgo

The Mexican War ended with the fall of Mexico City. All that remained was setting the terms of peace. Nicholas Trist began **negotiations** with the Mexican government. Trist and the Mexican leaders agreed to the Treaty of Guadalupe Hidalgo. Mexico gave up its northern provinces. In return the United States paid Mexico $15 million.

The United States gained more than half a million square miles of land as a result of the Mexican War. This included lands that today make up California, New Mexico, Nevada, Arizona, Utah, Wyoming,

The land that the United States gained from the Treaty of Guadalupe Hidalgo is known as the Mexican Cession.

United States Expansion in the Southwest

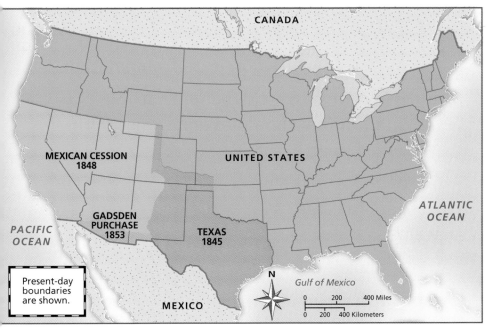

and Colorado. In 1853 the United States paid $10 million to Mexico for more land in the Southwest known as the Gadsden Purchase.

Life in the new territory soon changed. Thousands of Mexicans became United States citizens. American settlement grew, especially after gold was discovered in California in 1848. The country finally stretched from the Atlantic Ocean to the Pacific Ocean.

Glossary

annex to add or attach

boundary a line or natural feature that separates one area or state from another

manifest destiny the belief that the United States should expand west to the Pacific Ocean

negotiations the process of working with others to come to an agreement on an issue

province a territory governed by a country or empire

rebellion open and armed resistance to a government